mystery 3D LANDMARKS
Color by Number
On Black Paper

This Book Belongs to:

Test colors!

1. WHITE		**9.** PURPLE		**18.** DARK GREEN	
2. LIGHT ORANGE		**10.** VIOLET		**19.** TAN	
3. DARK ORANGE		**11.** LIGHT BLUE		**20.** LIGHT BROWN	
4. CREAM		**12.** SKY BLUE		**21.** BROWN	
5. RED		**13.** BLUE		**22.** DARK BROWN	
6. DARK RED		**14.** DARK BLUE		**23.** LIGHT GREY	
7. PINK		**15.** YELLOW GREEN		**24.** DARK GREY	
8. DARK PINK		**16.** OLIVE GREEN		**25.** BLACK	
		17. GRASS GREEN		**26.** YELLOW	

1. White

2. Light Orange

3. Dark Orange

4. Cream

5. Red

6. Dark Red

7. Pink

8. Dark Pink

9. Purple

10. Violet

11. Light Blue

12. Sky Blue

13. Blue

14. Dark Blue

15. Yellow Green

16. Olive Green

17. Grass Green

18. Dark Green

19. Tan

20. Light Brown

21. Brown

22. Dark Brown

23. Light Grey

24. Dark Grey

25. Black

26. Yellow

Please share
your results
with photos
as Feedback!
Highly
Appreciated!
Rate
Us!
★★★★★

1. White

2. Light Orange

3. Dark Orange

4. Cream

5. Red

6. Dark Red

7. Pink

8. Dark Pink

9. Purple

10. Violet

11. Light Blue

12. Sky Blue

13. Blue

14. Dark Blue

15. Yellow Green

16. Olive Green

17. Grass Green

18. Dark Green

19. Tan

20. Light Brown

21. Brown

22. Dark Brown

23. Light Grey

24. Dark Grey

25. Black

26. Yellow

Please share
your results
with photos
as Feedback!
Highly
Appreciated!
Rate
Us!

HINT FOR PREVIOUS:
2. BROOKLYN BRIDGE
NEW YORK CITY. USA

2. Light Orange

3. Dark Orange

4. Cream

5. Red

6. Dark Red

7. Pink

8. Dark Pink

9. Purple

10. Violet

11. Light Blue

12. Sky Blue

13. Blue

14. Dark Blue

15. Yellow Green

16. Olive Green

17. Grass Green

18. Dark Green

19. Tan

20. Light Brown

21. Brown

22. Dark Brown

23. Light Grey

24. Dark Grey

25. Black

26. Yellow

Please share
your results
with photos
as Feedback!
Highly
Appreciated!
Rate
Us!

★★★★★

2. Light Orange

3. Dark Orange

4. Cream

5. Red

6. Dark Red

7. Pink

8. Dark Pink

9. Purple

10. Violet

11. Light Blue

12. Sky Blue

13. Blue

14. Dark Blue

15. Yellow Green

16. Olive Green

17. Grass Green

18. Dark Green

19. Tan

20. Light Brown

21. Brown

22. Dark Brown

23. Light Grey

24. Dark Grey

25. Black

26. Yellow

Please share
your results
with photos
as Feedback!
Highly
Appreciated!
Rate
Us!

2. Light Orange

3. Dark Orange

4. Cream

5. Red

6. Dark Red

7. Pink

8. Dark Pink

9. Purple

10. Violet

11. Light Blue

12. Sky Blue

13. Blue

14. Dark Blue

15. Yellow Green

16. Olive Green

17. Grass Green

18. Dark Green

19. Tan

20. Light Brown

21. Brown

22. Dark Brown

23. Light Grey

24. Dark Grey

25. Black

26. Yellow

Please share
your results
with photos
as Feedback!
Highly
Appreciated!
Rate
Us!

★★★★★

1. White

2. Light Orange

3. Dark Orange

4. Cream

5. Red

6. Dark Red

7. Pink

8. Dark Pink

9. Purple

10. Violet

11. Light Blue

12. Sky Blue

13. Blue

14. Dark Blue

15. Yellow Green

16. Olive Green

17. Grass Green

18. Dark Green

19. Tan

20. Light Brown

21. Brown

22. Dark Brown

23. Light Grey

24. Dark Grey

25. Black

26. Yellow

1. White

2. Light Orange

3. Dark Orange

4. Cream

5. Red

6. Dark Red

7. Pink

8. Dark Pink

9. Purple

10. Violet

11. Light Blue

12. Sky Blue

13. Blue

14. Dark Blue

15. Yellow Green

16. Olive Green

17. Grass Green

18. Dark Green

19. Tan

20. Light Brown

21. Brown

22. Dark Brown

23. Light Grey

24. Dark Grey

25. Black

26. Yellow

HINT FOR PREVIOUS:
6. CASA MILA
BARCELONA, SPAIN

Please share
your results
with photos
as Feedback!
Highly
Appreciated!
Rate
Us!
★★★★★

1. White

2. Light Orange

3. Dark Orange

4. Cream

5. Red

6. Dark Red

7. Pink

8. Dark Pink

9. Purple

10. Violet

11. Light Blue

12. Sky Blue

13. Blue

14. Dark Blue

15. Yellow Green

16. Olive Green

17. Grass Green

18. Dark Green

19. Tan

20. Light Brown

21. Brown

22. Dark Brown

23. Light Grey

24. Dark Grey

25. Black

26. Yellow

1. White

2. Light Orange

3. Dark Orange

4. Cream

5. Red

6. Dark Red

7. Pink

8. Dark Pink

9. Purple

10. Violet

11. Light Blue

12. Sky Blue

13. Blue

14. Dark Blue

15. Yellow Green

16. Olive Green

17. Grass Green

18. Dark Green

19. Tan

20. Light Brown

21. Brown

22. Dark Brown

23. Light Grey

24. Dark Grey

25. Black

26. Yellow

HINT FOR PREVIOUS:
8. BERLIN WALL
BERLIN, GERMANY

1. White

2. Light Orange

3. Dark Orange

4. Cream

5. Red

6. Dark Red

7. Pink

8. Dark Pink

9. Purple

10. Violet

11. Light Blue

12. Sky Blue

13. Blue

14. Dark Blue

15. Yellow Green

16. Olive Green

17. Grass Green

18. Dark Green

19. Tan

20. Light Brown

21. Brown

22. Dark Brown

23. Light Grey

24. Dark Grey

25. Black

26. Yellow

HINT FOR PREVIOUS:
9. THE ARC DE TRIOMPHE
PARIS. FRANCE

Please share
your results
with photos
as Feedback!
Highly
Appreciated!
Rate
Us!

1. White

2. Light Orange

3. Dark Orange

4. Cream

5. Red

6. Dark Red

7. Pink

8. Dark Pink

9. Purple

10. Violet

11. Light Blue

12. Sky Blue

13. Blue

14. Dark Blue

15. Yellow Green

16. Olive Green

17. Grass Green

18. Dark Green

19. Tan

20. Light Brown

21. Brown

22. Dark Brown

23. Light Grey

24. Dark Grey

25. Black

26. Yellow

HINT FOR PREVIOUS:
10. THE REICHSTAG
BERLIN, GERMANY

Please share
your results
with photos
as Feedback!
Highly
Appreciated!
Rate
Us!
★★★★★

1. White

2. Light Orange

3. Dark Orange

4. Cream

5. Red

6. Dark Red

7. Pink

8. Dark Pink

9. Purple

10. Violet

11. Light Blue

12. Sky Blue

13. Blue

14. Dark Blue

15. Yellow Green

16. Olive Green

17. Grass Green

18. Dark Green

19. Tan

20. Light Brown

21. Brown

22. Dark Brown

23. Light Grey

24. Dark Grey

25. Black

26. Yellow

Please share
your results
with photos
as Feedback!
Highly
Appreciated!
Rate
Us!

★★★★★

1. White

2. Light Orange

3. Dark Orange

4. Cream

5. Red

6. Dark Red

7. Pink

8. Dark Pink

9. Purple

10. Violet

11. Light Blue

12. Sky Blue

13. Blue

14. Dark Blue

15. Yellow Green

16. Olive Green

17. Grass Green

18. Dark Green

19. Tan

20. Light Brown

21. Brown

22. Dark Brown

23. Light Grey

24. Dark Grey

25. Black

26. Yellow

HINT FOR PREVIOUS:
12. POMPEII
NAPLES, ITALY

2. Light Orange

3. Dark Orange

4. Cream

5. Red

6. Dark Red

7. Pink

8. Dark Pink

9. Purple

10. Violet

11. Light Blue

12. Sky Blue

13. Blue

14. Dark Blue

15. Yellow Green

16. Olive Green

17. Grass Green

18. Dark Green

19. Tan

20. Light Brown

21. Brown

22. Dark Brown

23. Light Grey

24. Dark Grey

25. Black

26. Yellow

1. White

2. Light Orange

3. Dark Orange

4. Cream

5. Red

6. Dark Red

7. Pink

8. Dark Pink

9. Purple

10. Violet

11. Light Blue

12. Sky Blue

13. Blue

14. Dark Blue

15. Yellow Green

16. Olive Green

17. Grass Green

18. Dark Green

19. Tan

20. Light Brown

21. Brown

22. Dark Brown

23. Light Grey

24. Dark Grey

25. Black

26. Yellow

HINT FOR PREVIOUS:
14. BOROBUDUR
MAGELANG, INDONESIA

Please share
your results
with photos
as Feedback!
Highly
Appreciated!
Rate
Us!

★★★★★

Please share
your results
with photos
as Feedback!
Highly
Appreciated!
Rate
Us!

★★★★★

1. White

2. Light Orange

3. Dark Orange

4. Cream

5. Red

6. Dark Red

7. Pink

8. Dark Pink

9. Purple

10. Violet

11. Light Blue

12. Sky Blue

13. Blue

14. Dark Blue

15. Yellow Green

16. Olive Green

17. Grass Green

18. Dark Green

19. Tan

20. Light Brown

21. Brown

22. Dark Brown

23. Light Grey

24. Dark Grey

25. Black

26. Yellow

HINT FOR PREVIOUS:
16. THE GREAT BUDDHA
OF KAMAKURA
KAMAKURA, JAPAN

Please share
your results
with photos
as Feedback!
Highly
Appreciated!
Rate
Us!

2. Light Orange

3. Dark Orange

4. Cream

5. Red

6. Dark Red

7. Pink

8. Dark Pink

9. Purple

10. Violet

11. Light Blue

12. Sky Blue

13. Blue

14. Dark Blue

15. Yellow Green

16. Olive Green

17. Grass Green

18. Dark Green

19. Tan

20. Light Brown

21. Brown

22. Dark Brown

23. Light Grey

24. Dark Grey

25. Black

26. Yellow

Please share
your results
with photos
as Feedback!
Highly
Appreciated!
Rate
Us!

1. White

2. Light Orange

3. Dark Orange

4. Cream

5. Red

6. Dark Red

7. Pink

8. Dark Pink

9. Purple

10. Violet

11. Light Blue

12. Sky Blue

13. Blue

14. Dark Blue

15. Yellow Green

16. Olive Green

17. Grass Green

18. Dark Green

19. Tan

20. Light Brown

21. Brown

22. Dark Brown

23. Light Grey

24. Dark Grey

25. Black

26. Yellow

**HINT FOR PREVIOUS:
18. TEMPLE OF THE SUN
PALENQUE, MEXICO**

Please share
your results
with photos
as Feedback!
Highly
Appreciated!
Rate
Us!

★★★★★

2. Light Orange

3. Dark Orange

4. Cream

5. Red

6. Dark Red

7. Pink

8. Dark Pink

9. Purple

10. Violet

11. Light Blue

12. Sky Blue

13. Blue

14. Dark Blue

15. Yellow Green

16. Olive Green

17. Grass Green

18. Dark Green

19. Tan

20. Light Brown

21. Brown

22. Dark Brown

23. Light Grey

24. Dark Grey

25. Black

26. Yellow

Please share
your results
with photos
as Feedback!
Highly
Appreciated!
Rate
Us!

★★★★★

1. White

2. Light Orange

3. Dark Orange

4. Cream

5. Red

6. Dark Red

7. Pink

8. Dark Pink

9. Purple

10. Violet

11. Light Blue

12. Sky Blue

13. Blue

14. Dark Blue

15. Yellow Green

16. Olive Green

17. Grass Green

18. Dark Green

19. Tan

20. Light Brown

21. Brown

22. Dark Brown

23. Light Grey

24. Dark Grey

25. Black

26. Yellow

**HINT FOR PREVIOUS:
20. GREAT WALL OF CHINA
BEIJING, CHINA**

Please share
your results
with photos
as Feedback!
Highly
Appreciated!
Rate
Us!
★★★★★

1. White

2. Light Orange

3. Dark Orange

4. Cream

5. Red

6. Dark Red

7. Pink

8. Dark Pink

9. Purple

10. Violet

11. Light Blue

12. Sky Blue

13. Blue

14. Dark Blue

15. Yellow Green

16. Olive Green

17. Grass Green

18. Dark Green

19. Tan

20. Light Brown

21. Brown

22. Dark Brown

23. Light Grey

24. Dark Grey

25. Black

26. Yellow

HINT FOR PREVIOUS:
21. THE RED FORT
DELHI, INDIA.

Please share
your results
with photos
as Feedback!
Highly
Appreciated!
Rate
Us!

★★★★★

1. White

2. Light Orange

3. Dark Orange

4. Cream

5. Red

6. Dark Red

7. Pink

8. Dark Pink

9. Purple

10. Violet

11. Light Blue

12. Sky Blue

13. Blue

14. Dark Blue

15. Yellow Green

16. Olive Green

17. Grass Green

18. Dark Green

19. Tan

20. Light Brown

21. Brown

22. Dark Brown

23. Light Grey

24. Dark Grey

25. Black

26. Yellow

**HINT FOR PREVIOUS:
22. SAGRADA FAMILIA
BARCELONA, SPAIN**

Please share
your results
with photos
as Feedback!
Highly
Appreciated!
Rate
Us!

2. Light Orange

3. Dark Orange

4. Cream

5. Red

6. Dark Red

7. Pink

8. Dark Pink

9. Purple

10. Violet

11. Light Blue

12. Sky Blue

13. Blue

14. Dark Blue

15. Yellow Green

16. Olive Green

17. Grass Green

18. Dark Green

19. Tan

20. Light Brown

21. Brown

22. Dark Brown

23. Light Grey

24. Dark Grey

25. Black

26. Yellow

Please share
your results
with photos
as Feedback!
Highly
Appreciated!
Rate
Us!

1. White

2. Light Orange

3. Dark Orange

4. Cream

5. Red

6. Dark Red

7. Pink

8. Dark Pink

9. Purple

10. Violet

11. Light Blue

12. Sky Blue

13. Blue

14. Dark Blue

15. Yellow Green

16. Olive Green

17. Grass Green

18. Dark Green

19. Tan

20. Light Brown

21. Brown

22. Dark Brown

23. Light Grey

24. Dark Grey

25. Black

26. Yellow

HINT FOR PREVIOUS:
24. MOUNT RUSHMORE
SOUTH DAKOTA, USA

Please share
your results
with photos
as Feedback!
Highly
Appreciated!
Rate
Us!

★★★★★

2. Light Orange

3. Dark Orange

4. Cream

5. Red

6. Dark Red

7. Pink

8. Dark Pink

9. Purple

10. Violet

11. Light Blue

12. Sky Blue

13. Blue

14. Dark Blue

15. Yellow Green

16. Olive Green

17. Grass Green

18. Dark Green

19. Tan

20. Light Brown

21. Brown

22. Dark Brown

23. Light Grey

24. Dark Grey

25. Black

26. Yellow

Please share
your results
with photos
as Feedback!
Highly
Appreciated!
Rate
Us!

1. White

2. Light Orange

3. Dark Orange

4. Cream

5. Red

6. Dark Red

7. Pink

8. Dark Pink

9. Purple

10. Violet

11. Light Blue

12. Sky Blue

13. Blue

14. Dark Blue

15. Yellow Green

16. Olive Green

17. Grass Green

18. Dark Green

19. Tan

20. Light Brown

21. Brown

22. Dark Brown

23. Light Grey

24. Dark Grey

25. Black

26. Yellow

Please share
your results
with photos
as Feedback!
Highly
Appreciated!
Rate
Us!

2. Light Orange

3. Dark Orange

4. Cream

5. Red

6. Dark Red

7. Pink

8. Dark Pink

9. Purple

10. Violet

11. Light Blue

12. Sky Blue

13. Blue

14. Dark Blue

15. Yellow Green

16. Olive Green

17. Grass Green

18. Dark Green

19. Tan

20. Light Brown

21. Brown

22. Dark Brown

23. Light Grey

24. Dark Grey

25. Black

26. Yellow

Please share
your results
with photos
as Feedback!
Highly
Appreciated!
Rate
Us!

2. Light Orange

3. Dark Orange

4. Cream

5. Red

6. Dark Red

7. Pink

8. Dark Pink

9. Purple

10. Violet

11. Light Blue

12. Sky Blue

13. Blue

14. Dark Blue

15. Yellow Green

16. Olive Green

17. Grass Green

18. Dark Green

19. Tan

20. Light Brown

21. Brown

22. Dark Brown

23. Light Grey

24. Dark Grey

25. Black

26. Yellow

1. White

2. Light Orange

3. Dark Orange

4. Cream

5. Red

6. Dark Red

7. Pink

8. Dark Pink

9. Purple

10. Violet

11. Light Blue

12. Sky Blue

13. Blue

14. Dark Blue

15. Yellow Green

16. Olive Green

17. Grass Green

18. Dark Green

19. Tan

20. Light Brown

21. Brown

22. Dark Brown

23. Light Grey

24. Dark Grey

25. Black

26. Yellow

**HINT FOR PREVIOUS:
29. EDINBURGH CASTLE
EDINBURGH, SCOTLAND**

Please share
your results
with photos
as Feedback!
Highly
Appreciated!
Rate
Us!

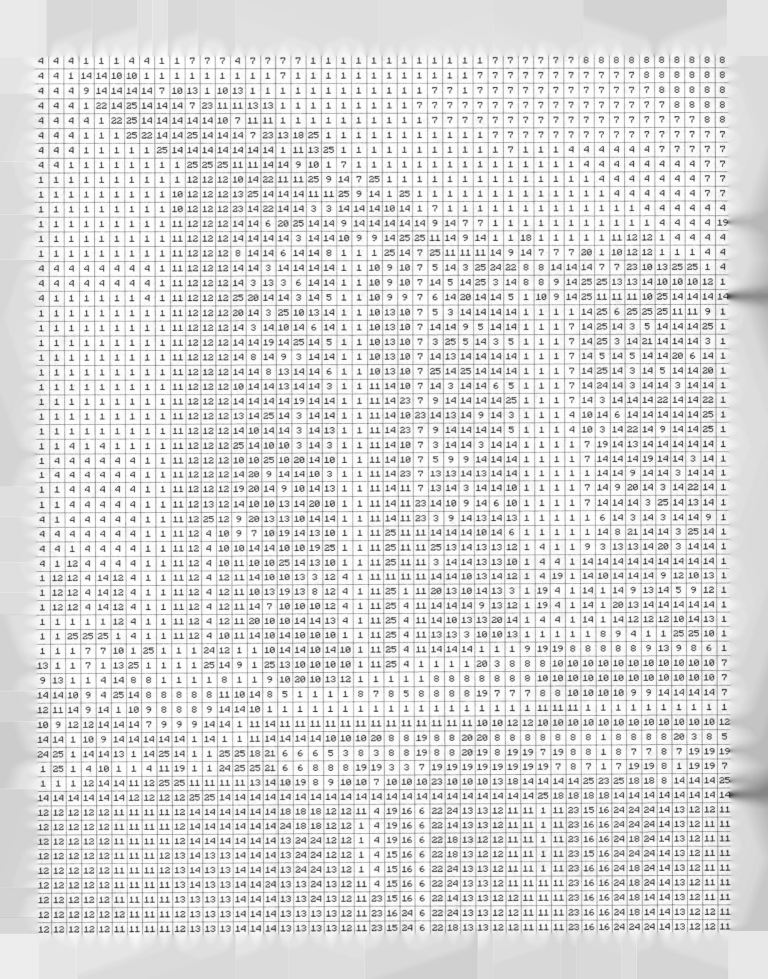

1. White

2. Light Orange

3. Dark Orange

4. Cream

5. Red

6. Dark Red

7. Pink

8. Dark Pink

9. Purple

10. Violet

11. Light Blue

12. Sky Blue

13. Blue

14. Dark Blue

15. Yellow Green

16. Olive Green

17. Grass Green

18. Dark Green

19. Tan

20. Light Brown

21. Brown

22. Dark Brown

23. Light Grey

24. Dark Grey

25. Black

26. Yellow

Please share
your results
with photos
as Feedback!
Highly
Appreciated!
Rate
Us!

★★★★★

1. White

2. Light Orange

3. Dark Orange

4. Cream

5. Red

6. Dark Red

7. Pink

8. Dark Pink

9. Purple

10. Violet

11. Light Blue

12. Sky Blue

13. Blue

14. Dark Blue

15. Yellow Green

16. Olive Green

17. Grass Green

18. Dark Green

19. Tan

20. Light Brown

21. Brown

22. Dark Brown

23. Light Grey

24. Dark Grey

25. Black

26. Yellow

HINT FOR PREVIOUS:
31. GRAND PALACE
BANGKOK, THAILAND

Please share
your results
with photos
as Feedback!
Highly
Appreciated!
Rate
Us!

★★★★★

1. White

2. Light Orange

3. Dark Orange

4. Cream

5. Red

6. Dark Red

7. Pink

8. Dark Pink

9. Purple

10. Violet

11. Light Blue

12. Sky Blue

13. Blue

14. Dark Blue

15. Yellow Green

16. Olive Green

17. Grass Green

18. Dark Green

19. Tan

20. Light Brown

21. Brown

22. Dark Brown

23. Light Grey

24. Dark Grey

25. Black

26. Yellow

HINT FOR PREVIOUS:
32. CHICHEN ITZA
YUCATAN, MEXICO

Please share
your results
with photos
as Feedback!
Highly
Appreciated!
Rate
Us!

★★★★★

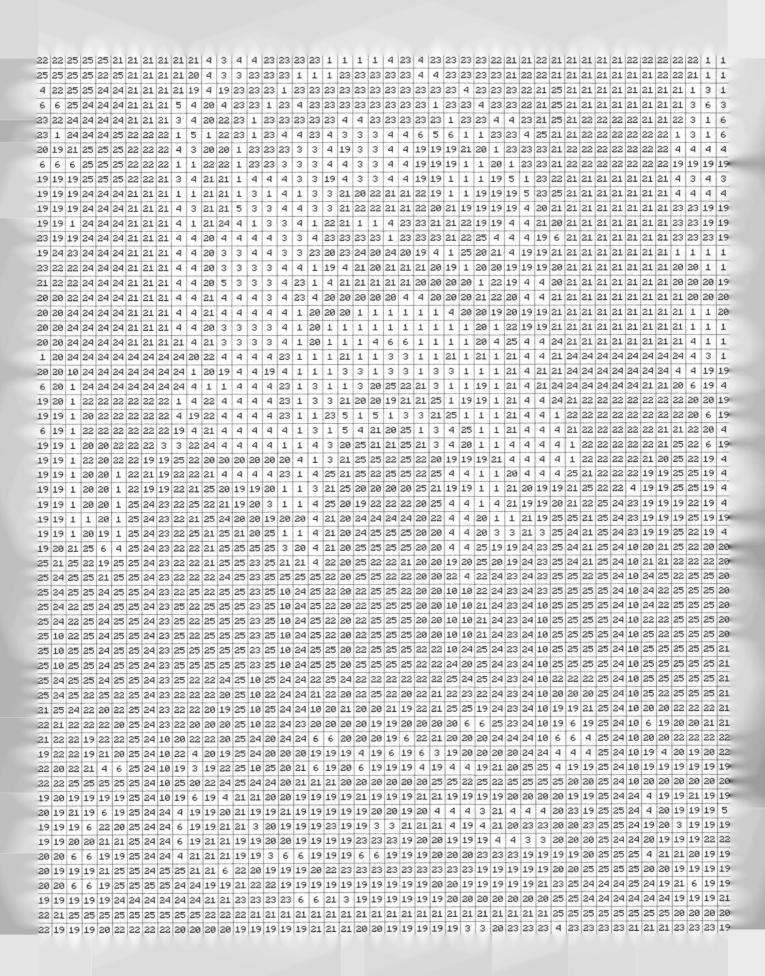

2. Light Orange

3. Dark Orange

4. Cream

5. Red

6. Dark Red

7. Pink

8. Dark Pink

9. Purple

10. Violet

11. Light Blue

12. Sky Blue

13. Blue

14. Dark Blue

15. Yellow Green

16. Olive Green

17. Grass Green

18. Dark Green

19. Tan

20. Light Brown

21. Brown

22. Dark Brown

23. Light Grey

24. Dark Grey

25. Black

26. Yellow

Please share
your results
with photos
as Feedback!
Highly
Appreciated!
Rate
Us!

1. White

2. Light Orange

3. Dark Orange

4. Cream

5. Red

6. Dark Red

7. Pink

8. Dark Pink

9. Purple

10. Violet

11. Light Blue

12. Sky Blue

13. Blue

14. Dark Blue

15. Yellow Green

16. Olive Green

17. Grass Green

18. Dark Green

19. Tan

20. Light Brown

21. Brown

22. Dark Brown

23. Light Grey

24. Dark Grey

25. Black

26. Yellow

HINT FOR PREVIOUS:
34. CN TOWER
TORONTO, CANADA

1. White

2. Light Orange

3. Dark Orange

4. Cream

5. Red

6. Dark Red

7. Pink

8. Dark Pink

9. Purple

10. Violet

11. Light Blue

12. Sky Blue

13. Blue

14. Dark Blue

15. Yellow Green

16. Olive Green

17. Grass Green

18. Dark Green

19. Tan

20. Light Brown

21. Brown

22. Dark Brown

23. Light Grey

24. Dark Grey

25. Black

26. Yellow

HINT FOR PREVIOUS:
35. HOOVER DAM
NEVADA/ARIZONA, USA

Please share
your results
with photos
as Feedback!
Highly
Appreciated!
Rate
Us!

1. White

2. Light Orange

3. Dark Orange

4. Cream

5. Red

6. Dark Red

7. Pink

8. Dark Pink

9. Purple

10. Violet

11. Light Blue

12. Sky Blue

13. Blue

14. Dark Blue

15. Yellow Green

16. Olive Green

17. Grass Green

18. Dark Green

19. Tan

20. Light Brown

21. Brown

22. Dark Brown

23. Light Grey

24. Dark Grey

25. Black

26. Yellow

HINT FOR PREVIOUS:
36. SPACE NEEDLE
SEATTLE, USA

Please share
your results
with photos
as Feedback!
Highly
Appreciated!
Rate
Us!

2. Light Orange

3. Dark Orange

4. Cream

5. Red

6. Dark Red

7. Pink

8. Dark Pink

9. Purple

10. Violet

11. Light Blue

12. Sky Blue

13. Blue

14. Dark Blue

15. Yellow Green

16. Olive Green

17. Grass Green

18. Dark Green

19. Tan

20. Light Brown

21. Brown

22. Dark Brown

23. Light Grey

24. Dark Grey

25. Black

26. Yellow

Please share
your results
with photos
as Feedback!
Highly
Appreciated!
Rate
Us!

2. Light Orange

3. Dark Orange

4. Cream

5. Red

6. Dark Red

7. Pink

8. Dark Pink

9. Purple

10. Violet

11. Light Blue

12. Sky Blue

13. Blue

14. Dark Blue

15. Yellow Green

16. Olive Green

17. Grass Green

18. Dark Green

19. Tan

20. Light Brown

21. Brown

22. Dark Brown

23. Light Grey

24. Dark Grey

25. Black

26. Yellow

Please share
your results
with photos
as Feedback!
Highly
Appreciated!
Rate
Us!
★★★★★

1. White

2. Light Orange

3. Dark Orange

4. Cream

5. Red

6. Dark Red

7. Pink

8. Dark Pink

9. Purple

10. Violet

11. Light Blue

12. Sky Blue

13. Blue

14. Dark Blue

15. Yellow Green

16. Olive Green

17. Grass Green

18. Dark Green

19. Tan

20. Light Brown

21. Brown

22. Dark Brown

23. Light Grey

24. Dark Grey

25. Black

26. Yellow

HINT FOR PREVIOUS:
39. PANAMA CANAL
PANAMA CITY, PANAMA

Please share
your results
with photos
as Feedback!
Highly
Appreciated!
Rate
Us!

1. White

2. Light Orange

3. Dark Orange

4. Cream

5. Red

6. Dark Red

7. Pink

8. Dark Pink

9. Purple

10. Violet

11. Light Blue

12. Sky Blue

13. Blue

14. Dark Blue

15. Yellow Green

16. Olive Green

17. Grass Green

18. Dark Green

19. Tan

20. Light Brown

21. Brown

22. Dark Brown

23. Light Grey

24. Dark Grey

25. Black

26. Yellow

HINT FOR PREVIOUS:
40. CHRIST THE KING
LISBON, PORTUGAL

Please share
your results
with photos
as Feedback!
Highly
Appreciated!
Rate
Us!
★★★★★

2. Light Orange

3. Dark Orange

4. Cream

5. Red

6. Dark Red

7. Pink

8. Dark Pink

9. Purple

10. Violet

11. Light Blue

12. Sky Blue

13. Blue

14. Dark Blue

15. Yellow Green

16. Olive Green

17. Grass Green

18. Dark Green

19. Tan

20. Light Brown

21. Brown

22. Dark Brown

23. Light Grey

24. Dark Grey

25. Black

26. Yellow

Please share
your results
with photos
as Feedback!
Highly
Appreciated!
Rate
Us!

1. White

2. Light Orange

3. Dark Orange

4. Cream

5. Red

6. Dark Red

7. Pink

8. Dark Pink

9. Purple

10. Violet

11. Light Blue

12. Sky Blue

13. Blue

14. Dark Blue

15. Yellow Green

16. Olive Green

17. Grass Green

18. Dark Green

19. Tan

20. Light Brown

21. Brown

22. Dark Brown

23. Light Grey

24. Dark Grey

25. Black

26. Yellow

HINT FOR PREVIOUS:
42. SHEIKH ZAYED
GRAND MOSQUE
ABU DHABI, UAE

Please share
your results
with photos
as Feedback!
Highly
Appreciated!
Rate
Us!

★★★★★

2. Light Orange

3. Dark Orange

4. Cream

5. Red

6. Dark Red

7. Pink

8. Dark Pink

9. Purple

10. Violet

11. Light Blue

12. Sky Blue

13. Blue

14. Dark Blue

15. Yellow Green

16. Olive Green

17. Grass Green

18. Dark Green

19. Tan

20. Light Brown

21. Brown

22. Dark Brown

23. Light Grey

24. Dark Grey

25. Black

26. Yellow

Please share
your results
with photos
as Feedback!
Highly
Appreciated!
Rate
Us!

1. White

2. Light Orange

3. Dark Orange

4. Cream

5. Red

6. Dark Red

7. Pink

8. Dark Pink

9. Purple

10. Violet

11. Light Blue

12. Sky Blue

13. Blue

14. Dark Blue

15. Yellow Green

16. Olive Green

17. Grass Green

18. Dark Green

19. Tan

20. Light Brown

21. Brown

22. Dark Brown

23. Light Grey

24. Dark Grey

25. Black

26. Yellow

Please share
your results
with photos
as Feedback!
Highly
Appreciated!
Rate
Us!

★★★★★

2. Light Orange

3. Dark Orange

4. Cream

5. Red

6. Dark Red

7. Pink

8. Dark Pink

9. Purple

10. Violet

11. Light Blue

12. Sky Blue

13. Blue

14. Dark Blue

15. Yellow Green

16. Olive Green

17. Grass Green

18. Dark Green

19. Tan

20. Light Brown

21. Brown

22. Dark Brown

23. Light Grey

24. Dark Grey

25. Black

26. Yellow

Please share
your results
with photos
as Feedback!
Highly
Appreciated!
Rate
Us!

1. White

2. Light Orange

3. Dark Orange

4. Cream

5. Red

6. Dark Red

7. Pink

8. Dark Pink

9. Purple

10. Violet

11. Light Blue

12. Sky Blue

13. Blue

14. Dark Blue

15. Yellow Green

16. Olive Green

17. Grass Green

18. Dark Green

19. Tan

20. Light Brown

21. Brown

22. Dark Brown

23. Light Grey

24. Dark Grey

25. Black

26. Yellow

**HINT FOR PREVIOUS:
46. WASHINGTON MONUMENT
WASHINGTON, D.C., USA**

Please share
your results
with photos
as Feedback!
Highly
Appreciated!
Rate
Us!

2. Light Orange

3. Dark Orange

4. Cream

5. Red

6. Dark Red

7. Pink

8. Dark Pink

9. Purple

10. Violet

11. Light Blue

12. Sky Blue

13. Blue

14. Dark Blue

15. Yellow Green

16. Olive Green

17. Grass Green

18. Dark Green

19. Tan

20. Light Brown

21. Brown

22. Dark Brown

23. Light Grey

24. Dark Grey

25. Black

26. Yellow

1. White

2. Light Orange

3. Dark Orange

4. Cream

5. Red

6. Dark Red

7. Pink

8. Dark Pink

9. Purple

10. Violet

11. Light Blue

12. Sky Blue

13. Blue

14. Dark Blue

15. Yellow Green

16. Olive Green

17. Grass Green

18. Dark Green

19. Tan

20. Light Brown

21. Brown

22. Dark Brown

23. Light Grey

24. Dark Grey

25. Black

26. Yellow

1. White

2. Light Orange

3. Dark Orange

4. Cream

5. Red

6. Dark Red

7. Pink

8. Dark Pink

9. Purple

10. Violet

11. Light Blue

12. Sky Blue

13. Blue

14. Dark Blue

15. Yellow Green

16. Olive Green

17. Grass Green

18. Dark Green

19. Tan

20. Light Brown

21. Brown

22. Dark Brown

23. Light Grey

24. Dark Grey

25. Black

26. Yellow

Please share
your results
with photos
as Feedback!
Highly
Appreciated!
Rate
Us!

Made in the USA
Las Vegas, NV
12 December 2024

13949493R00057